Poems for Meditation
An Invitation to Prayer

Antoinette Voûte Roeder

apocryphile press
BERKELEY, CA

Apocryphile Press
1700 Shattuck Ave #81
Berkeley, CA 94709
www.apocryphile.org

© 2014 Antoinette Voûte Roeder
ISBN 9781940671482
Printed in the United States of America.

"Morning Wind" is used with permission of the copyright holder, Coleman Barks. I found this version in *A Year with Rumi: Daily Readings* (New York: HarperCollins, 2006). It was originally published in *The Essential Rumi* (New York: HarperCollins, 1995).

Photographs by Michael Thomas Roeder.

All rights reserved. No part of this book may be reproduced, stored in a retrieval system, or transmitted in any form or by any means—electronic, mechanical, photocopy, recording, or otherwise—without written permission of the author and publisher, except for brief quotations in printed reviews.

Contents

To the reader 5

Breath Prayer 9

Sound Prayer 47

Prayer 67

Appendix I: Facilitating Breath Awareness 92

Appendix II: About Contemplative Prayer 95

Acknowledgements 99

About the author 100

It is with deep gratitude that I dedicate
this volume of poetry to
Tante Cile and Tante Cor, my Sufi guides
James Finley, my Christian contemplation teacher
Shunryu Suzuki and Will Johnson,
my Buddhist meditation teachers.

To the reader

If you are a contemplative, you take time to look, to listen, and in those, to love. We do the same in contemplative prayer only inwardly. Each is part of one movement. What begins inwardly must *out*, what begins outwardly must *in*. What separates *in* and *out* is a semi-permeable membrane and is in the end perhaps merely illusion.

Writing about this kind of prayer is like trying to catch lightning. Every poem in this collection is only an approximation of the experience itself. It is the proverbial finger pointing at the moon, not the moon itself.

These poems were inspired by my daily reading of *A Year With Rumi*, Coleman Barks' collection of Rumi poems, one for every day of the year. At least, I suspect they were. I am not conscious of any intention to write such poems, they just started coming one day as I was sitting in meditation and just as mysteriously departed some nine months later.

I sit on a prayer cushion in front of a small altar-like table on which I have placed various articles, many given to me by dear friends. I pray in the company of these friends. They are my community. The articles are as diverse as feathers, stones, bits of driftwood, and the Jewish text of the Shema in a lovely little mezuzah. A Christian prayer hangs on the wall above the table as well as a photograph of a statue of the seated Buddha clad in a crown and shawl of snow.

When I sit in prayer, I begin with a brief reading, often a poem, sometimes scripture or some other spiritual reading. I ring a gong that is actually a deep-toned brass bowl tapped with a small mallet. Following the teachings of my mentor James Finley, I gently place my attention with my breath. By gently placing my attention with my breath I give the ever-active mind something to do while I sink deeper into prayer.

"Gently" is the operative word in this prayer. Even the words "focus" and "concentration" are muscle-words. They trample the experience of accompanying the breath. The relationship with breath is so delicate (for relationship is what it is until at last we indwell the breath and it us) that all that is needed is a disinterested and very light glance. Breath itself takes it from there. To breathe is to be: it is without goal, has no ambition or pride. No muscular effort is required, no need for fancy tools or furnishings. We have our breath with us always until we breathe our last and our breath returns to the One who gave it to us.

It is common knowledge that we will be plagued by distractions of all kinds, thoughts, memories, sounds, physical discomfort. That is why we befriend our breath or a prayer word or both. The important thing is our intention, commitment and faithfulness. As Shunryu Suzuki (*Zen Mind, Beginner's Mind*) says so simply, just to sit [in meditation] is enough. Bring your self in all sincerity. Come. Be. It is easy. It is hard. Come any way.

When I first settle into meditation and feel myself in my body, these words form in my mind: "Here I am." (1 Samuel 3:4) This is the most powerful commitment I can make: to be here, to gather to myself all the bits I've lent out or thought lost, the good, bad, and ugly, and then to drop into my breath and let it breathe me into wholeness, into greater being. It is more than I can ask for.

My breath is the gateway to my body. I become fully aware of every limb, every digit. With grace even the subtlest movement within is felt and noticed. Yet nothing is judged, nothing is rejected, nothing is even labelled. All is simply noticed.

This is contemplative prayer. It is Christian, as attested to by the great mystics of this tradition. It is common to other faith traditions as well, often referred to as meditation. We are all invited into contemplative prayer. If we have prayed all our lives with words and images, at some point we will be led into a deeper experience of the Holy when words and images dry up.

Contemplative prayer is surely a profound experience of hospitality, receptivity, and entrusting. We welcome the Holy, we welcome ourselves, we open ourselves to what the Spirit has for us, and we entrust ourselves wholly to Presence in this moment now.

*****

We live on a small man-made lake which is visited by all kinds of waterfowl, especially in migratory season. Some poems will speak of the presence of water, of rain, of birds as they live just outside my window and inhabit my prayer as surely as I do.

These poems come from a place that does not distinguish among faith traditions. In my experience, contemplation does not recognize anything but the deep longing for wholeness that is always being offered to us. Sometimes certain words will be capitalized. This is the poet's attempt to indicate the Holy Other in personal experience. It is a paradox of mystery and intimacy and can never be just one or the other.

The reader/pray-er may like to skip around in this collection as the Spirit leads. However the poems are organized somewhat according to theme. Section I: Breath Prayer. Section II: Sound Prayer. Section III: Prayer.

These small poems are intended as a prelude to prayer. I would suggest reading only one or two at a time. May they be a blessing.

—*Antoinette Voûte Roeder*

"...the opening lines of the Book of Genesis introduce the divine Breath (*ruah*) that lies at the basis of all being and all life, that power which gives everything its form and shape. 'In the beginning God created the heavens and the earth. Earth was without form and void, and darkness was upon the face of the deep, and the Breath of God was moving over the face of the waters' (Gen. 1:1-2)."

—Ruben L. F. Habito, *Healing Breath:
Zen Spirituality for a Wounded Earth*

* * * * *

"The morning wind spreads its fresh smell.
We must get up to take that in,
that wind that lets us live.
Breathe, before it's gone."

—Coleman Barks, "Morning Wind,"
A Year With Rumi: Daily Readings

Breath Prayer

Soon as I fold
my legs under me
I hear the word
welcome

Every cell dances
with anticipation
in the dusky dawn
awareness casts

I vowed to begin
every prayer with thanks

So I come, Beloved
gratitude quickening
coursing through my body
ascending my breath
staining my lips
bowing my head
in the multiplicity
and anguish
of embodied life

My breath
offers up words
I have not asked for

Unbidden prayer

Thank you

No tools, no methods
Simplicity itself

Life stripped down
to its essence

sit
connect
breathe

What is this work I do,
sitting, breathing?

I am a gate
by which Breath
enters the world.

Linger in the shadows
Watch from the margins
Rest in the pauses

Hush

Life
reveals
herself
here

Is there
anything more delicious
than breathing?

What is
the Buddha's
half-smile
about?

Could it be

he tastes
the sweetness
of his own breath?

What a luxury it is
to breathe

Sometimes
breath arrives quietly
pauses
curls back
a wave
lapping the
shore

Sometimes breath
breaks into pieces
sharp shards shaking
inside and out

All times
breath
serves life

Sometimes my breath
disappears
like mist rising
from a lake
leaving the waters
untroubled
still
reflective

Meditating
with a fine rain
slipping down my back

my breath
a waterfall

What are blessings made of?

Cool air
through an open window
midst summer's heat

Blue heron
scarcely visible
among the reeds

My body dropping
into gravity's lap

Breath
unimpeded

At the end of each exhale
a small death awaits

It lies there
quiet
dark
comforting

The early morning dark
embraces me

my breath
my only light

In the watercolor dawn
my breath moves
like a small mist
over the water

mystery
all its own

I am
a tiny kayak
floating down
the Amazon of
my breath

Sitting back
in my body
I sip my breath
from Your cup

I am home

Breathe
on the mirror
of my soul

that I might find
my face within Yours

Listen to the wind
blowing between
the covers of
the world

The wind, my breath
swirls seductively
throughout my body
animating every cell

With the very next exhale
the Other may appear

When breath
turns to champagne
in my mouth
every cell
in my body
swoons with
delight

What is prayer?

"I let my breath
make love to me."

What is love?

"It is prayer."

When I sit
in meditation
mouth full of
my own sweet breath

who is the Beloved?

O Lord

I am
a harp string
strung taut
in a sanctuary
of silence
Each time I enter
here, it shivers
into life, sends small
shocks throughout the dark,
sparking vibrations all along
its length

Music for Your ears alone

When you exhale
wait with patience
upon the Holy

Another layer
will be revealed

Breath

Exquisite

Sometimes
in the midst of
my breath
I become
a million specks
of awareness
gathered here
on this cushion

I am
no more
no less
than the wild grass
that bends in the wind
of Sacred Breath

Your breath
is my poem

My spine is like
the soaring mast
of a tall ship
in love with
the wind

sails filled
surrendered to
the journey

Sometimes my breath
scrapes my throat
like dry twigs

My spine creaks
as it shifts
in gravity's grasp

Sometimes Rumi
makes no sense
at all!

My breath rises slowly
-a dancer
spreading her arms-
fills the sky
then drops into folds,
soft and quiet
before
beginning again

Sometimes
upon the long descent
of my breath
the beat of my heart
comes into view

Sometimes I remember
to thank it

Beneath
my breath
a steady pulse
a faithful drum

Not always
will it be so

Breathing
is
all
there
is

until
it
is
over

Then
some thing
else

When my last breath
rolls away and
every thing breaks open

Tell me I am free
and
never
let
me
go

Sound Prayer

The gong
is just the gate

If you cling to it
you will miss
what awaits you

life beyond duality

Follow
the sound
of the gong
and you will find
your self in paradise

I rang the gong
but did not hear it

Only its memory
rests on the air

Even when
the gong's sound
has truly disappeared

there is still
a round rolling
of the air

My breath
is locked
in the cage
of my ribs

With the sound
of the gong
the bars
fall away
open to
breath-full
space

There is a moment
when the gong's sound swells,
hangs suspended in
the belly of the air
encloses me
diffuses
and disappears

Shimmers of sound
grow in circles
from the center
of the gong

I listen
till I can hear
no more

This sound
now dwells
in another sphere

The sound of the gong
fills my head
is already traveling
through my veins

perhaps has always
been there

The gong's sound enters
my chest's center
turns its bright side
then its dark
in continuous exchange

two partners
in a dance
that spills and spirals
throughout time

I feel the tone
of the gong
its rounded waves
oscillating

my skin responsive
as to
a lover

This time
the gong's tone travels
up my back
touching every
vertebra, stopping at
the sternum where
it opens to
the world: the Russian
steppes, an Indian market,
a bomb explosion in Israel,
waves lapping on
a distant shore and I,
present to all

The gong's tone
passes in wisps
and curls out
the open window

I sit alone

A tuning fork
a weather vane
know nothing of
the inner wind
that vibrates
every nerve
with the sound
of the gong

The gong's sound
enters my open
hands

Vibrations meet
and blend

The skin is but
a membrane,
thin and fine,
clothing all
vibration

The gong's full sound
impermanent
like everything else
fades
escapes my open window
leaves delicious silence

Wake up!

Listen

Once the gong
has sounded
it travels forth
to meet universal sound
which is the same

There is no end
no beginning

I am gone
in the fast disappearing
sound of
the gong

Alice
down the rabbit hole

Sound the gong
it shimmers
diffuses
billows into edgeless clouds
and gathers in my cells
a living golden column where
my spine used to be

A Poet's Question

In my waning years
will I only respond
like a gong when it is struck?

Will I no longer
originate sound?

Prayer

For years
I listened to
teachers of all kinds,
some wise

Now I turn
to the teacher within,
the one who knows me
altogether

Every morning
I meet my heart

It is green
and darkly pulsing

It tells me my story

It has no words

I listen

All my efforts,
resistance, defenses
are laid aside

in prayer
I am innocent
new
knowing
known

Open the door!
Let me in!

Whose door
is it?

Is there a door?

On my prayer table
stones and feathers
angels and sacred text

Below
the world's carnage,
broken bones

Both belong

When I sit here
with my chest torn open
my heart spills out
to all the world

a wound
I would not close

Cool are
the prayer stones
in my hands

Hot is
the passage
to my heart

If you cannot say it
straight and simple
like the arrow's
flight off the bow
then breathe,
just
breathe

Release your grip
on this wheelbarrow
of words

Watch it roll away
as you lift off

Free at last

My thoughts are
a vine flowing over
an old stone wall,
rain slipping down
a window pane,
dew dripping off
the fronds of a fir

Nothing permanent

When I am
in this state

Don't come at me
with cutting words
with sharp glances

Can you not tell?

I am wearing
my inside outside

Does Silence know herself?

Does she plumb the depths
of her ineffable Being
in stillest light,
in lightest dark?

Or does she have
need of *me*, I who have
knowledge of sound,
I who savor her,
reflect her back
to herself?

The wind sighs through the trees

Sometimes
when my breath has dropped
to its deepest point
stillness creeps like mist
over my soul
ushering in
silence

Even silence expands
admits something else

I think I hear the universe
humming on its axis
wheeling through space

Sometimes beyond that
the silence of the Constant
before all beginnings
listening
with me

When you enter
that kernel of Silence
there is no longer
a you and I,
just Life
living Itself

In meditation
I ride the circle
of Infinity

Then
there
is Infinity
only

In the darkened room
rain, so slight I cannot
hear it, moistens my
lips, my cheeks, mists
my eyes

You
I see clearly

You bathe me
in soft sunlight

All my body
becomes fluid

Flows to join
all creation

These shimmers and shudders
are just a foretaste,
aren't they?

The deep darkness of
the wedding night
is still to come

I'm growing my spine
Beloved

With each breath
another vertebra grows
into a rung
on Jacob's ladder

On every rung
a flower blooms

When Elijah
was taken up
into heaven
chariot and all,
was it
an act of love,
this explosive one-ing,
erasing boundaries
and distinctions in
one ecstatic leap?

Keep no one
outside the circle
of your prayer

Not the cast-off
lover, not the friend
turned cold, not the
estranged brother

There is nothing
to fear. All
are here.

Prayer Group

There was a moment
when we fell into
the heart of stillness,
completely surrendered,
and a clock
stopped ticking
at the center
of the world.

Whether you've knelt
in prayer
every day of your life
or never
sunk to your knees
you will not be
honoured more
nor less

The blessing
comes now
and now
and
now

Final Prayer

Let me ride
my last long lingering
breath like a swan
sailing beneath
the arched bridge of
the world
smoothly
effortlessly
out
to the open sea.

Appendix I

Facilitating Breath Awareness

There are many ways to become more aware of the breath. We tend to take breathing for granted and when we first start noticing our breath, we may find we are trying hard to control it. And so I suggest sidling up to it, as it were, or just watching it out of the corner of your eye.

What I have learned about the breath has come chiefly from yoga. The following is one way to start noticing your breath. Intentional breathing is a powerful thing. One can quickly raise all kinds of energy so I caution you to only do what feels comfortable and safe. If six complete breaths feel like too much, reduce it to four or two. Take three breaths from deep within the body and on the inhalation, retain it at three different places in the body: this you will be able to feel. I retain it at the base of the diaphragm, again at the high sternum, then at the top of the inhalation. Then I expel the breath in one long swoop. Take a moment to breathe normally. Then do the same again, only on the exhalation this time. Suspend the breath first around the heart level, then lower in the body, then expel it altogether, three times. By this time you will feel alert, clear, and ready to settle into paying attention to your breath quietly.

I discovered the following way myself. Once you have settled into your meditation posture take three intentionally slow, big breaths. Imagine taking the first breath from your tailbone up the back, let it expand the ribs and spiral around in there as it travels up through the shoulder blades and through the crown of the head. Then let it cascade down like a waterfall, like a baptism of sorts. With the second breath, imagine taking it from your pubic bone up the front of the body, swirling through the belly and the diaphragm before proceeding through the sternum, the throat, and up through the center of your forehead, then out of the crown of the head. Again, let it wash over you. Take the third long breath from your central core and let it do what it wants. Do not direct it.

Now you will have already touched in on your natural breathing. Step away from the focused intentional breathing and let your breath breathe you. This is very subtle. The tendency to want to direct the breath will remain. Keep stepping back from it and welcome your breath as it wants to come to you. Trust that Breath will breathe you and you will join it, joining Universal Breath, joining the Breath of Creation at the root of the world. Relax into its height, its breadth, its depth and know yourself both held and carried.

Appendix II

About Contemplative Prayer

Many of us learned to pray from a family member or in church. We learned particular prayers by rote: table graces, bedtime prayers, The Lord's Prayer. We learned to petition, to offer praise and thanks, and to intercede for others and ourselves. If we continued to live with prayer as part of our lives, chances are that at some point our prayer experience changed radically. Like everything else in life, prayer is not static. The Spirit is always on the move (John 3:8).

St. John of the Cross has described this process clearly. When familiar prayer breaks down we may be thrown into a time of great unease, bewilderment, loss. Our prayers stick between our teeth. Words desert us. The Scriptures have lost their meaning. Worst of all, we fear that God has gone missing. Why should we even continue to pray?

This is a time when it is truly beneficial to meet with a spiritual director or soul friend who knows the path and recognizes the signs. What is happening is actually a very natural development in our spiritual journey. It is a breakdown of our concepts of who God is and how God operates. It happens every time we become too comfortable in our relationship with the Holy, as shown throughout the Hebrew Scriptures. When we think we have God in our pockets and at our command, we have to be prepared for a shock. If God is always about the "more," as I've learned from the Jesuits, then this is God's way of telling us that God now wants to reveal God's Self in a different manner, a process that will continue until the end of our days.

Contemplative prayer is what I like to call "bare bones" prayer. It is prayer stripped of all images and words. Contemplation, as I learned to define it in my spiritual direction education, means "to gaze upon, to behold, with love." The change from discursive prayer (prayer with words) to contemplative prayer can come abruptly or slowly over time. When words fail us we know we are being called into contemplation. This is when we learn to listen. If we have talked throughout our prayers, it may be quite disconcerting to fall into the silence that contemplative prayer offers. We may question whether this is prayer at all. Even though we may hear nothing but silence, we have to trust that this is from God. Meister Eckhart said, "Silence is the language of God." Thomas Keating adds, "Anything else is a bad translation." Instead of pelting the Holy with our words, we open our hands and our hearts to receive. We wait upon God.

Silence is uncomfortable for many of us. A lull in conversation finds us scurrying for another topic. There will be a period of adjustment to the prayer of silence. In addition, the moment we drop into silence we are assailed by a mind that won't stop thinking. We cannot turn the chatter off. And we don't need to. The mind is made for thinking; it is gift. So we give it something to do. We can place our attention with our breathing. Or we can introduce a prayer word or mantra. A prayer word can be something from Scripture. We can ask for a prayer word. We can use it in conjunction with our breathing. Or we can do what Benedictine John Main teaches, and simply repeat the prayer word over and over until it fades away. Cistercian priest Thomas Keating only introduces the prayer word when thoughts have once more abducted us. As prayer deepens these "tools" will fade away and Breath will breathe itself.

I was introduced to breath prayer by Anthony de Mello and James Finley. It felt like coming home. The moment we start paying attention to our breath it is as if all the stage lights come on at once. The body is illuminated. Breath oxygenates the blood and the blood circulates throughout our bodies, animating every cell. We become aware of sensations on the skin, under the skin, in the muscles, even in our organs. Involuntary movement may occur. This is the body responding to the quickening that is taking place within. We are incarnate beings, we are embodied. Contemplative prayer is integrative prayer.

We in the west have tended to dissociate from our physical selves, an unfortunate product of the Enlightenment that emphasized intellectual knowing. The Christian tradition has tended to find fault with the flesh, and a patriarchal society has not helped. Even now when we exercise we likely do it *to* our bodies or *for* our bodies, sometimes to the point of pain. We have yet to discover that we *are* our bodies and our bodies are sacred. There are body practices which enhance meditation and awareness. Tai Chi, Hatha Yoga, and Qi Gong are only a few of those.

We bring our whole selves to prayer, body, breath, soul, spirit. The work is God's. All we can do is cultivate the ground and show up, open, receptive, with loving hearts.

A great deal has been written about contemplative prayer. To learn more, these are some authors to consult: William Barry, Anthony Bloom, Ruth Burrows, James Finley, Thomas Green, Thomas Keating, Martin Laird, Thomas Merton, William Shannon, Francis X. Tuoti. Of these authors, Thomas Merton is possibly the best known and most prolific on the subject of contemplative prayer. He stood on the shoulders of those mystics who came before him: Teresa of Ávila, St. John of the Cross, the Rhineland mystics, and the anonymous work called *The Cloud of Unknowing*.

Acknowledgements

Special thanks go to poet Susan McCaslin for her careful reading of and insightful suggestions for an earlier version of the manuscript.

I appreciate very much Will Johnson's enthusiastic response to the manuscript's first draft.

Erin Michie, with her yoga expertise, suggested some important changes to the appendix dealing with breath awareness. Thank you for your invaluable advice, Erin.

Nancy Roeder, my favourite grammar police, made helpful suggestions for the appendices. Thank you, Nan.

My daughter Sasha Roeder Mah, in her capacity as editor and proof reader, gave the entire text her expert perusal. Thanks so much, Sasha.

Maxine Cowan, Elisabeth Rinsoz, and Glenda Sartore read and commented on the manuscript.

I am very grateful to John Mabry and the staff at Apocryphile Press for their patience with and support of my work over the years. You people make beautiful books!

I am deeply grateful to you all. Your support, encouragement, and friendship mean the world to me.

About the poet

ANTOINETTE VOÛTE ROEDER was born in The Netherlands and is twice an immigrant: first to the United States as a child, later to Canada with her husband and two children.

Her paternal grandmother was Anabaptist, her grandfather atheist. Her aunts adopted Sufism, the mystical branch of Islam. Her parents were Church of England (i.e. Anglican). The poet grew up with the mystery of the Eucharistic celebration and grew into the Beloved of Sufism by way of literature and poetry. She is rooted in the Christian tradition which is rich with mystics. She reads widely and finds the Holy everywhere.

Antoinette's degrees are in music. She is a trained spiritual director and has an active spiritual direction practice. In addition she offers retreats in the area of writing and spirituality. She has been writing poetry since she was 15. Her previous books are *Weaving the Wind* and *Still Breathing*. Antoinette lives in Edmonton, Alberta, Canada.

www.ingramcontent.com/pod-product-compliance
Lightning Source LLC
Chambersburg PA
CBHW022107040426
42451CB00007B/170